Everybody Needs a Barnabas

Creating a Culture of Encouragement in the Local Church

Danny Sinquefield

Copyright 2025

All rights reserved

ISBN: 979-8-9902665-3-7

WeServePublishing.org

Unless otherwise stated all Scripture verses quoted are from the New King James Version ®, Copyright © 1982 by Thomas Nelson, Inc. Used by permission.

Dedication

This book is dedicated to the ministry staff and members of Faith Baptist Church in Bartlett, Tennessee. It was my joyful privilege to serve as pastor of Faith for nearly three decades. The principles I share in this book were learned and lived out while serving this dear church family.

With gratitude, I also dedicate this book to the Barnabas brothers in my life who believed in me and gave me opportunities to become a pastor and leader in the local church and beyond:

- Nathan Blackwell, our youth minister in my home church, LaBelle Haven Baptist in Memphis, Tennessee

- Don Minshew, my partner in church planting at Lake Forest Baptist in Walls, Mississippi

- Dr. Virgil Lovett, my pastor at Trinity Baptist in Apopka, Florida

- Dr. Randy Davis, my friend and executive director of the Tennessee Baptist Mission Board

I especially want to express my deep love and appreciation to my wife, Rhonda—for her constant encouragement and ministry partnership. Thank you, sweet bride of my youth, for always believing, always praying, and always sharing life and ministry with me! Your love has challenged, sustained, and made me a better man. I'm grateful for your friendship beyond words.

IV

CONTENTS

Foreword — VII

Introduction — IX

Chapter 1: What's in a Name? — 01

Chapter 2: Joyful Generosity — 07

Chapter 3: Going to Bat for Others — 13

Chapter 4: Seeing the Grace of God — 19

Chapter 5: Getting in the Game — 25

Chapter 6: When Conflicts Happen — 33

Chapter 7: Jesus, Our Ultimate Encourager — 39

Epilogue — 45

Acknowledgements — 47

Foreword

Everybody Needs a Barnabas is a biography, a history lesson, a church-growth manual, and a heartwarming call to action for anyone seeking to live an impactful life.

In a world marked by discouragement, division, and disillusionment, Dr. Danny Sinquefield offers a blueprint for a better way—a path filled with joy, dedicated to advancing God's kingdom. Through these pages, he paints a vivid picture of a life well-lived, grounded in the transformative power of encouragement.

Drawing from Scripture, Danny highlights numerous examples of the life-changing encouragement Barnabas provided to Paul, Mark, Luke, and others. We can all recall moments of despair when we were ready to give up, only to have a Barnabas enter our lives, speak words of hope, offer support, and inspire us to press on. Through this book, Danny embodies that same Barnabas Spirit.

In nearly fifty years of ministry, I have faced moments of discouragement and despair that could have led me to abandon the pastorate. Yet, in those valleys, God sent individuals who poured courage into my heart, urging me to "stay by the stuff" and continue onward.

Imagine a church where every pew is filled with a Barnabas—believers who uplift and inspire one another. God has blessed me with the privilege of pastoring such churches, where sweet fellowship thrives, Christ-followers grow, spiritually lost individuals find salvation, and worship is authentic. These are hallmarks of a church culture saturated with biblical encouragement.

Everybody Needs a Barnabas was written by a man who radiates encouragement as freely as the University of Tennessee's Pride of the Southland Band plays "Rocky Top" at a football game. For nearly three decades, Danny led his church to embody the Barnabas Spirit. His credibility, character, and competence make him uniquely qualified to write about building a culture of encouragement.

I love this book, and I love its author. Thank you, dear friend, for blessing our lives with *Everybody Needs a Barnabas*.

Randy C. Davis
President and Executive Director
Tennessee Baptist Mission Board

Introduction

Imagine a church family that is saturated with spirit-filled members who truly love and look after one another—where every person is valued, encouraged, cared for, and treated as significant. Let that image stir your heart for your local congregation. It is a beautiful snapshot of the Early Church that began at Pentecost, subsequently impacted the entire city of Jerusalem, and eventually influenced the whole world with the message of Jesus.

Something beautiful and powerful happens when God's people receive encouragement. The opposite is also true. When God's people are discouraged—isolated and separated from fellowship with other believers—something bleak and broken happens. This is too often the reality in church today. Brethren, these things ought not be so.

The spiritual climate of many churches in twenty-first century American culture has drifted far from the first century mindset and model. Leaders are discouraged and often wonder if change will come. Is there any hope for a renewal and spiritual awakening in the Church of our generation? Keep reading if you believe the answer is yes!

When his brother returned from Jerusalem with news that the walls of the city were still broken down and the gates still destroyed from fire, Nehemiah was overcome with anguish. God's people were in great trouble (Nehemiah 1:3), and this caused his heart grief. He knew that the way things were in his day were not the way things were supposed to be. And, with God's help, things could be made right. That same sense of anguish, commitment, and determination is the drive we need to trust the Lord for a transition and transformation in our day.[1]

The book you are holding in your hands has been written from my heart. It is born out of a belief similar to that of Nehemiah's: that God wants *more* for His Church and His people. The Lord's desire is for the Church to be alive with joy, hope, and a compelling sense of purpose, and for every member to be encouraged, equipped, and empowered in serving the Lord.

---

[1] The destruction happened decades before—when Babylon invaded—which God allowed because of the Kingdom of Judah's persistent sin. Though we know from Scripture that negative consequences result from sin, my analogy does not go so far as to imply that the state of the Church today is purely a result of sin.

I once heard Dr. Adrian Rogers, the well-known pastor of Bellevue Baptist Church in Memphis, Tennessee, say, "There is no such thing as a small church. Every church is a mission outpost of Almighty God!" Those words resonate in my spirit to this day. I believe that it is possible for every local church to become a strong, thriving, and reproducing body of believers who are encouraged to be encouragers!

It is true that we are living in a day of widespread discouragement for pastors, leaders, and church members alike. However, God's Word provides a beautiful solution as demonstrated by the life and ministry of Joseph of Cyprus—also known as Barnabas in Scripture. This, of course, is a nickname that captures his character as the "Son of Encouragement." Every person needs a friend like Barnabas, and every church can develop a culture of encouragement by following a few biblical principles that trace the life and ministry of this "good man, full of the Holy Spirit and of faith" (Acts 11:24).

The story of Barnabas only appears in the Bible a handful of times, but his influence is woven into the fabric of the New Testament. It is not an exaggeration to say that Barnabas's life influenced the writings of Mark, Luke, and Paul. As a result, his shadow still exists large today. Each mention of Barnabas in the Bible is significant and serves as a major principle for application in the life of the local church. For instance, the first time we meet Joseph of Cyprus in Acts 4, he is practicing joyful generosity in giving to the Lord's work. This principle would saturate the ministry of the Early Church and is still the root of our mission giving today.

Following the foregrounding chapter of the book, each chapter highlights a specific attribute that Barnabas displays in every biblical account he appears in. These qualities include generosity, vision, humility, vulnerability, deference, integrity, faithfulness, and godly conflict resolution. These chapters each contain a list of application points and discussion questions to use in discipleship settings or small groups, or for personal leadership development. Finally, the ultimate encourager, the Lord Jesus, is highlighted as the supreme example for God's people.

Read on, friend, and be encouraged!

CHAPTER ONE

What's in a Name?

A good name is to be chosen rather than great riches, Loving favor rather than silver and gold. (Proverbs 22:1)

Sometimes, a nickname sticks. It just fits and feels right. That is exactly what happened with a man named Joses, or Joseph, in the first-century church. In Acts 4:36, he is introduced in a compelling statement as "Joses, who was named Barnabas by the apostles (which is translated Son of Encouragement), a Levite of the country of Cyprus." The writer Luke captures the character of Barnabas in this concise introduction.

Nicknames can be humorous, like the guy in the joke named Lucky, who had no legs, one eye, and one ear. They can also be sarcastic, like a man called Tiny, who was six feet, eight inches tall and weighed over 400 pounds. But in the case of Joseph of Cyprus, the name given to him perfectly reflected his character and his conduct. He was an encourager. He poured courage into others and put other people in a position to succeed. His story is revealed through only a handful of biblical references, but in each, he appears in the role of an encourager.

> *Joses, who was named Barnabas by the apostles (which is translated Son of Encouragement), a Levite of the country of Cyprus.*

The biblical name Barnabas (Son of Encouragement) translates literally to "one who comes alongside" to comfort, exhort, or to encourage. He was named and known by his spiritual gift—encouragement.[2] That is exactly what this good man did at every opportunity—so much so that his real name (Joses or Joseph), though good, is nearly forgotten in history. But the name Barnabas lives on as a beautiful reminder of the man who made such a tremendous impact on the Early Church and whose influence lives on today. In fact, while Barnabas never wrote a single book of the Bible, his fingerprints can be traced through nearly half of the New Testament. His personal ministry with Saul of Tarsus (the Apostle Paul), with Luke (author of the Gospel of Luke and the Book of Acts), and with John Mark (author of the Gospel of Mark) are legendary.

---

[2] R. Kent Hughes, *Preaching the Word: Acts* (Crossway Books, 1996), 72.

That introductory verse mentions a few other critical details of Barnabas's life. He was a Levite from the country of Cyprus. A Levite is a minister in the Jewish tradition (a descendent of the tribe of Levi) whose role was to serve in the Synagogue. So, this man was an encourager who served. He probably heard the Gospel of Jesus when he visited Jerusalem at Pentecost. Perhaps he was among the 3,000 souls who were saved as a result of Peter's sermon recorded in Acts 2. One thing is for certain: Barnabas was a man who was marked by the Gospel. His relationship with Jesus began a lifelong journey of ministry to others and service to the Lord that impacts God's Kingdom to this very day. He spent his entire life modeling Jesus, who "did not come to be served, but to serve" (Mark 10:45).

This book is about more than a man with a good name. It is designed to help create a culture of encouragement in the local church. Imagine how healthy and how helpful it would be for your church to have encouragers at every age level and in every area of ministry! The opportunities for creating a ministry of encouragers are endless.

Not everyone can sing, play an instrument, or teach a class. Only a few will be called to pastor or serve as vocational missionaries. But every single believer can be an encourager. It is certainly a skillset and a calling, but there are character qualities of Barnabas's ministry that can be taught and caught as they are modeled in the context of the local church.

The Great Need for Encouragers

If there was ever a time for a renewed ministry of encouragement in our churches, it is now. The theme for God's people to "encourage one another" is woven throughout the Scriptures. So much of Paul's writing, for example, emphasizes this admonition. It is quite possible that Barnabas's influence in Paul's life was in mind when he challenged the churches in Galatia: "Therefore, as we have opportunity, let us do good to all, especially to those who are of the household of the faith" (Galatians 6:10). The concept of "doing good to all" is at the core of the Barnabas ministry—to encourage others and bring out the best in other people.

We are living in a day of widespread discouragement. Our culture has shifted from a *caring community of neighbors* who develop deep relationships on the front porch to people who are communicating primarily in a cyber-world behind screens and with electronic devices. Too many of our local churches are struggling with symptoms that mirror this culture. We have a generation of young people and adults who are devoid of social skills due to the lack of real-life interpersonal relationships. Conversations with one another are limited to a few characters in a text or an emoji reply on social media platforms. As a result, people are hungry for a human touch. This is true both in both the lives of pastors and the people of the Church. Many members of our congregations are battling isolation, loneliness, discouragement, and depression.

Unfortunately, not every church makes all people feel welcome. They don't always communicate a sense that people (visitors or members) are wanted or needed. It is entirely possible for a person to be in a large room filled with people and still have an overwhelming sense of being all alone. This is a heart-breaking reality that must be addressed in our generation. No pastor or leader of a local congregation would ever want that to be true of their church.

I am suggesting that it is the absence of the Barnabas Spirit that causes such a lack of connection in the local church—but the good news is that something can be done. This small book offers help that will assist in creating a culture of encouragement that can change the experience of every person who is a member or a guest in your church. Establishing a renewed sense of the Barnabas Spirit will promote the sense of belonging, ministry purpose, and connection that is so needed in our generation. We have an opportunity to embrace these biblical principles and begin this process in our churches moving forward.

Defining the Barnabas Spirit

Sometimes things are best described by their absence. That is certainly true of the Barnabas Spirit in the life of a local church. You know it when you don't see it! Perhaps a feeling of being overlooked or ignored has been your experience while attending a small group or a church service as a guest. No one welcomed you or inquired about your name and your story. No one attempted to make a friendly connection before, during, or after your visit. In a very real sense, you may have felt worse after the visit than if you had not attended at all. I can imagine that every church wants to correct and develop the intentionality of human interaction.

Most churches need to be constantly reminded that they are in the people business. The Barnabas Spirit is marked by intentional interaction with real people, and it creates a culture of encouragement and permeates every area of ministry within the local church. This is true of any church of any size. When a local congregation embraces the mindset of the Barnabas Spirit, they embrace intentionality and become more people-focused.

Each chapter of this book will deal in more detail with the life and ministry of Barnabas as documented in the Book of Acts. However, the essence of the Barnabas Spirit can be summed up by the twin concepts of the Great Commandments—love God and love people (Matthew 22:36–40)—and the Great Commission—make disciples of all people (Matthew 28:18–20). As church leaders focus more on their mission and their message, they will be more prepared to develop the Barnabas Spirit in the life of their church.

Developing the Barnabas Spirit

The local church is the perfect gathering place to activate this ministry of encouragement. It can happen in small groups or with individual discipleship encounters. Your church can become a laboratory for developing a Barnabas ministry among members. Here are a few ideas for getting started in your church. The key is connecting everyone with an area of ministry that allows them to encourage others.

- Enlist a group of volunteers who will be responsible for writing birthday cards to members. The goal here is to give a personal touch in communicating a caring spirit.

- Begin a couple to couple ministry in your church that pairs older married couples with a younger couple to meet once a month for a meal and to share life together—allowing the older couple to offer the wit and wisdom developed over a lifetime of following Jesus.

- Pay attention to young people, single adults, and senior adults coming to church alone. Reach out and invite them into the small group Bible studies or age-related activities of the church.

- Train individual members to touch base—by phone or in person—with members who have been missing from your church.

- Encourage deacons and elders to be sensitive to marginalized people in the congregation. No one should be excluded, sit by themselves, or eat at a table alone. Show kindness to people on the edges.

- Create a first impression ministry for your church that enlists friendly members to serve on the front lines of contact with people. They may welcome people as they enter the building, pass out bulletins, or serve at the welcome center, directing individuals and families to specific ministry areas (nursery, children's classes, worship locations, etc.).

- Enlist members who can bake cookies or homemade bread to do so and give these away to guests, shut-in members, and senior adults.

- Create ministries for gathering and serving a meal for families when someone is sick, has come home from the hospital, or is grieving the death of a loved one.

- Use your imagination for getting every member involved at some level of a ministry of encouragement.

The Encouragers in Your Life

It is always helpful to follow the advice of the old hymn and "count your many blessings, name them one by one"[3] regarding the people who have served as a

---

[3] Johnson Oatman, Jr., "Count Your Blessings." *The Baptist Hymnal* (Convention Press, 1956), 318.

Barnabas in your life. The list may include a teacher, a coach, a youth ministry leader, or any number of possibilities. Take a minute and think about the people who have spoken positively and invested personally in your life.

Ask the Lord to bring to your mind those key encouragers in your Christian journey. Consider the character qualities of their lives—some were subtle, and others were more overt, but each one served as a Barnabas in your life. Give thanks to the Lord for their ministry and ask God to allow you the privilege of serving others in a similar way.

I am overwhelmed with gratitude for the many individuals who have served as a Barnabas in my life. My introduction to the Barnabas Spirit began early in my Christian journey with a local church during my teen years. I was discipled by an array of people including Sunday school teachers, student ministry leaders, and peers.

The Lord placed godly men in my life who encouraged, supported, corrected, and modeled the Christian life in practical ways. I was challenged to grow in God's Word and given opportunities to serve in the local church as a young teen, share my faith with others, and live on mission as a lifestyle. All of these experiences took place in the context of a local church.

The conviction to write this book and to share these principles was born out of the biblical conviction that each member of the Church is a valuable part of the beautiful Body of Christ. Paul's reminder to the believers in Corinth is clear: "God has set the members, each one of them, in the body just as He pleased. And if they were all one member, where would the body be? But now indeed there are many members, yet one body" (1 Corinthians 12:18–20). There is no insignificant member, and we truly need each other to be a whole, healthy church family.

Questions for Discussion

1. What is the definition of the "Barnabas Spirit?"

2. How can a church create opportunities for individuals to serve as a Barnabas?

3. Who in your life has encouraged you along the way?

4. What is the Lord saying to you so far in this study?

5. Why is the ministry of encouragement in the life of the Church so important?

CHAPTER TWO

Joyful Generosity

So let each one give as he purposes in his heart, not grudgingly or of necessity; for God loves a cheerful giver. (2 Corinthians 9:7)

Encouragers are generous people. They readily give their time, openhandedly share their resources, and willingly serve others—asking nothing in return. Following a brief introduction to Barnabas in Acts 4, Luke captures the generous nature of his character: "having land, [he] sold it, and brought the money and laid it at the apostles' feet" (Acts 4:37). What an amazing beginning to the story of a man who continues to make a Kingdom impact in the lives of God's people 2,000 years later!

This reference to the gracious, giving spirit of Barnabas is foundational to the Early Church's focus on sacrificial giving. The concept of joyful generosity takes root here, in this testimony of Barnabas, and it continues bearing eternal fruit throughout history. In this chapter, we will discover how the thread of joyful generosity modeled by this good man manifests itself through the early days of the Church and how it can still be embraced by every member of our day.

The first principle in rightly understanding the concept of joyful generosity is that it involves more than just money. The key to cultivating a mindset of encouragement among members is to create a generous way of living. This principle is best understood when they see it modeled. When the congregation hears stories of generosity and celebrates those stories in the context of worship, something powerful begins to happen. This spirit of Barnabas-style generosity becomes contagious, and the discipline is embraced more widely in the Church.

God's Word is clear: "The generous soul will be made rich, And he who waters will also be watered himself" (Proverbs 11:25). Dr. Bill Elliff eloquently captures this idea of joyful generosity in his article, "The Glorious Blessing of Generosity," writing, "Everything you have came from Him. Everything. The generous man knows this and sees himself merely

> *"Everything you have came from Him. Everything. The generous man knows this and sees himself merely as a steward charged to faithfully do what God desires with God's resources. It's his great joy to do so and the Father's great pleasure to bless a generous man."*

7

as a steward charged to faithfully do what God desires with God's resources. It's his great joy to do so and the Father's great pleasure to bless a generous man."[4]

Barnabas and the Macedonian Mindset

When the Apostle Paul wrote to encourage the Corinthian believers to become even more generous in their mission giving, he illustrated the idea using the Macedonian churches. In 2 Corinthians 8, Paul literally calls out the lack of generosity in Corinth when he contrasts their generosity to the generous believers we know as the churches of Thessalonia, Berea, and Philippi.

Demonstrating generosity throughout his life, Barnabas's spirit of generosity spread and influenced these small congregations. God used Barnabas to touch the life of Saul of Tarsus, who touched the life of so many others. So although these churches most likely never met Barnabas, they experienced his generous heartbeat through the teaching and preaching of Paul. Had it not been for Barnabas, the missionary journeys may have never occurred.

The pattern Paul mentions in this classic passage is the Macedonians giving *beyond* their ability (v. 3), they gave with much *urgency* (v. 4), and they gave *themselves* first to the Lord (v. 5). As a result, the Holy Spirit produced a supernatural generosity among members of the church. Their gifts to the mission offering for the suffering saints in Jerusalem became legendary. Imagine how the spiritual temperature in your church would change if people began to sense a sudden desire to give and to serve with renewed urgency!

Servant leaders have a way of producing other authentic servant leaders. While this characteristic of Barnabas is covered in greater detail in subsequent chapters, it is worth mentioning this truth of reproduction here as well. In their book, *Calling Out the Called,* authors Scott Pace and Shane Pruitt devote an entire chapter on serving others. This reminder is worth noting: "Many churches and ministries have some great servant leaders. If you find a healthy church who has a good minister, you will know it. You can hear the evidence of that leader in their voices and see it in the lives of others. The effects of a good servant leader can be felt for generations to come."[5]

Joyful generosity is motivated ultimately by a heartfelt love for Jesus. When Paul issued this challenge, he reminded the Corinthians of the beautiful gift of the Savior. He writes, "For you know the grace of our Lord Jesus Christ, that though He was rich, yet for your sakes He became poor, that you through His poverty might become rich" (2 Corinthians 8:9). Barnabas is certainly a good example, but the

---

[4] Bill Elliff, "The Glorious Blessing of Generosity," *Graceful Truth,* August 16, 2023, https://billelliff.org/blogs/news/the-glorious-blessing-of-generosity.
[5] Scott Pace and Shane Pruitt, *Calling Out the Called* (B&H Publishing, 2022), 121–122.

ultimate expression of generosity is found perfectly in the life, love, sacrifice, and ministry of the Lord Jesus. This beautiful reminder from the Apostle Paul should motivate God's people to be the most caring, gracious, giving, compassionate, and generous people on the planet!

The Generous People of God

There are people in most every congregation who are blessed with a generous spirit and the grace of giving. These members model the Barnabas Spirit of generosity as they give their time, spiritual gifts, and personal resources to the Lord in the context of ministry through the local church. Every pastor knows the blessing of shepherding people who are generous.

The discipline of generosity can also be developed over time. Through biblical teaching on the subject and celebrating the stories of generosity, the congregation can be challenged to new levels of sharing, giving, and serving.

> *The discipline of generosity can also be developed over time. Through biblical teaching on the subject and celebrating the stories of generosity, the congregation can be challenged to new levels of sharing, giving, and serving.*

I encourage other pastors to teach and preach periodically on biblical texts related to storehouse tithing, grace giving, and living generously. On one occasion as I was preaching through a series on stewardship, a member of the church invited me to a breakfast meeting. He informed me that he had been listening carefully to the messages and had concluded that the teaching on tithing was correct. As a result, he became convicted that although he and his wife were generous givers, they had not been practicing tithing. He shared that he had recently sold one of his businesses and he now intended to give a tithe to the Lord from this resource. Right there in the middle of a small breakfast shop, this member informed me that his gift would be over $2 million to the budget of the church. In moments like those, a pastor can only *act like* he has been there before—and respond with a grateful spirit!

One man in our congregation, Mr. Tom Day, is investing his retirement years discipling and counseling others. He literally pours his life into other men as a personal ministry. On one occasion, Mr. Tom and I hosted several young ministry leaders on a personalized trip to the Holy Land. He basically funded the entire experience as an investment in the ministry of the young men. His legacy of joyful generosity will far outlive his time on the earth.

Not everyone can give a huge financial gift like these examples. But everyone can give generously at some level. Some will even find unusual and creative ways to give to the Lord's work.

Our modern churches are in desperate need of champions like Barnabas who model joyful generosity. Historically, it is the people of God who have demonstrated compassion, hope, and help in communities across the nation and around the world. Wherever you find disaster, tragedy, suffering, hunger, and human need, the people of God have been on the frontlines serving in Jesus's name.

Leaders who model this mindset will be amazed by the influence of their generous spirit on the members of their church and beyond. As a young teenager attending church alone, I experienced others taking notice that I needed a little extra encouragement from time to time. Adults in my life offered kind expressions of support and assistance. God brought generous, caring people into my life at just the right time. I'm not sure how they knew about my situation, but they always seemed to be aware that I could use financial assistance for camps, college tuition, and mission trips. Through them, I saw the Barnabas Spirit firsthand. Being the recipient of such kind expressions of generosity has fostered that spirit in my life—one that my wife and I continue to model in our life together.

Here are a few ideas for churches and individuals about how to apply the spirit of generosity to others:

- Pay attention to children and students who attend church alone and offer to provide assistance for camps, mission trips, and other ministry opportunities that may require funding. This can often be done anonymously.
- Seek out college students who may be struggling with the cost of tuition and book expenses and assist financially at whatever level you can. Providing even one student with a little help is a wonderful example of Barnabas-style generosity.
- Give generously through your church's budget and mission offerings to exemplify a desire to impact the Kingdom through your local church.
- Be faithful in serving through the various ministries of your local church and encourage others to join you.
- Keep your passport updated and always be prepared to say "yes" to any opportunity for mission and ministry involvement.
- Ask the pastor if there are any needs that he is aware of in the congregation or in the community and offer to lead that effort by providing service or support.

Giving God Our Very Best

The overarching teaching from Scripture related to stewardship is that God *desires* our very best, and He also *deserves* our very best. This truth is dramatically illustrated during the days of the prophet Malachi in the final book of the Old Testament. God's people were not only *not* being generous, but they were also not being thankful. In fact, they openly expressed an unthankful and ungrateful attitude toward God. This reflected a contemptible spirit by the people giving blind and lame animals as their sacrifice offering. God responded to this unthankful and ungrateful style of worship by saying it would be better for someone to "shut the door" of the temple rather than continue to disrespect His name with such unfit sacrifices (Malachi 1:7–10).

> *The overarching teaching from Scripture related to stewardship is that God desires our very best, and He also deserves our very best.*

Sadly, people today often offer God only their spare time and their spare change. In our day, the Church is sometimes treated like a Salvation Army or a Goodwill drop off post. People donate what has become useless or things they no longer want or need. How many old pianos, for example, have been given to the Church because its donor has purchased a new one? But what if that habit suddenly shifted and God's people offered brand-new items to the Lord's work and kept the old ones instead? We will never see a revival in our churches or in our land by offering God our leftovers. And the Church can create this shift, praying for more of the very best to be given to the Lord and acting on that prayer.

The Barnabas Spirit of joyful generosity is exactly the opposite of Malachi's day. It embraces the deep realization that God in fact is worthy of our very best time, service, and resources. From this reality, people in the Church with the spirit of Barnabas will become role models of generous giving and living. They will express it in humility and with a sense of urgency. The Church is blessed beyond words by such champions who demonstrate the heart of Barnabas in joyful generosity—which I have had the opportunity to witness as a pastor of one local church for nearly twenty-eight years.

The stories of sacrificial giving from our "little country church" are those of which legends are made. On several occasions, I had the privilege of seeing several families in our church choose to give of themselves by strengthening an inner-city church on Sunday mornings and by going out to start new churches when there was a need. Our church's people purchased an old campground and saw the Lord bring it back to life and become a vibrant Gospel-focused ministry. The people of the church prioritized pouring into young pastors and setting them up for success. As a result, that church trained and launched ministry leaders, leaving fingerprints all across the country and around the world.

My prayer is for God to send a supernatural spiritual awakening to His people as we prayerfully seek His face and turn from our wicked ways. Let us give God our very best for the rest of our days. The Church that God uses to change the world will be one that is permeated by this beautiful generous, joyful spirit.

Questions for Discussion

1. Describe and define the biblical concept of "joyful generosity."

2. Read about the churches in Macedonia (2 Corinthians 8) and share insights gained from this text.

3. How can a person practice the Barnabas Spirit of generosity in practical ways?

4. In what ways has your life been directly impacted by the generosity of others?

5. How can God's people avoid falling into the disrespectful mindset that is described in Malachi?

CHAPTER THREE

Going to Bat for Others

Let nothing be done through selfish ambition or conceit, but in lowliness of mind let each esteem others better than himself. Let each of you look out not only for his own interests, but also for the interests of others. (Philippians 2:3–4)

Encouragers care about other people. They often advocate for and promote the success of others. Sometimes they see potential in people that others struggle to recognize. This beautiful characteristic shows up early and often in the life and ministry of Barnabas. No doubt, the Apostle Paul never forgot this pivotal moment in his own life—when Barnabas went to bat for him.

> Encouragers care about other people. They often advocate for and promote the success of others. Sometimes they see potential in people that others struggle to recognize.

The profound impact it had on Paul motivated him to model and teach this principle throughout his lifetime. Paul was deeply impacted by this heart-searing lesson, and he would spend the rest of his ministry replicating this principle in others. Barnabas believed in Saul of Tarsus, and he risked his own reputation to prove it.

The story is told in a few brief verses in Acts 9. Leaders of the Early Church who gathered in Jerusalem had suffered serious pushback from the Jewish establishment as well as from Roman officials. There was mounting pressure to cease and desist from following and teaching about the Rabbi from Nazareth. Peter and John had been arrested (Acts 4), and Stephen had been killed (Acts 7). But those courageous leaders of the Early Church declared, "We cannot but speak the things which we have seen and heard" (Acts 4:20). So quitting was not really an option for those newly energized first-century followers of Jesus.

However, when a recent convert with the reputation of a feared persecutor of the Church appeared on the scene, they were understandably concerned. At first, no one believed that Saul was trustworthy or authentic in his new dramatic profession of faith. For them, it was only reasonable to assume that Saul could not be trusted. They feared it was a trap—or worse. Perhaps they would be arrested, imprisoned, or stoned to death like their friend Stephen.

The conversation among those Early Church leaders must have been quite intense. Jesus was reported to have confronted Saul of Tarsus on the road to Damascus (Acts 9:1–9). After that monumental encounter, Saul surrendered his life to the Lord Jesus and was radically transformed. His heart and life were forever changed. He would later write about this heart transformation in a clear definition of the Gospel. Paul declared in that well known verse that "if any man is in Christ, he is a new creation; old things are passed away and all things become new" (II Corinthians 5:17).

Taking a Risk on an Unknown

At this point, Barnabas became involved in the conversation. Acts 9:26 states clearly the concern of the church leaders: "And when Saul had come to Jerusalem, he tried to join the disciples; but they were all afraid of him, and did not believe that he was a disciple."

Imagine this moment: Saul was trying to join this church, but he didn't have enough votes. That's a church business meeting that wasn't going well! Years later, perhaps the disciples talked about the "what if" consequences of that moment. What if Saul had been excluded from joining the church? What if he had never become Paul the Apostle? What if Barnabas never sent for him to come to Antioch? What if there had never been those missionary journeys to take the Gospel to the world? But as they say, the rest is history!

The story told in Acts 9 is golden. It reveals one of the most significant aspects of the Barnabas Spirit. The Early Church leaders took a huge risk on this relatively unknown, new believer in that meeting. Their decision is now legendary. But in that moment, it was a serious test of faith—both for Barnabas and the others.

In a simple but profound statement, we read, "But Barnabas took him" (Acts 9:27a). Wow. Barnabas *took* Saul. So much weight hangs in that simple phrase. Over half of the New Testament was written by this untested, unproven individual. His history was sketchy, to say the least. His reputation was certainly not attractive. There was no good reason to vote for him. But Barnabas *took* Saul.

I remember those long, sweltering summer days growing up when kids played outside until dark. One of the favorite games in our neighborhood was baseball— usually played in our backyard. As one of the youngest kids in the group, I can still feel that shaky anxiety when the captains were picking teams. My big brother, Mike, was almost always one of the captains. I remember the excitement and sense of belonging when my brother called my name to be on his team. I wasn't the strongest, or fastest, or the best player—but he chose me. Even a younger brother needs a Barnabas!

And think about our ultimate Advocate—the Lord Jesus. When there was no good reason for Him to do so, He *chose* us: "just as He chose us in Him before the foundation of the world, that we should be holy and without blame before Him in love" (Ephesians 1:4). He *adopted* us: "having predestined us to adoption as sons by Jesus Christ to Himself, according to the good pleasure of His will" (Ephesians 1:5). And He has *accepted* us: "to the praise of the glory of His grace, by which He made us accepted in the Beloved" (Ephesians 1:6).

Barnabas went to bat for the same man who wrote each of these sweet promises. Not only did Barnabas *take* Saul, he also *brought* him to the disciples and *declared* to them details concerning his amazing transformation (Acts 9:27). He represented Saul and spoke positively on his behalf. In that moment, Barnabas was demonstrating one of the most beautiful aspects of his character. He truly cared for others. He saw the potential in Saul when others could only see their own fears and strong feelings. Barnabas believed in Saul even when others had their doubts. He pushed another into the spotlight of ministry rather than seize the moment for himself. What a champion of God's grace we see in this incredibly unselfish moment!

> *Barnabas believed in Saul even when others had their doubts. He pushed another into the spotlight of ministry rather than seize the moment for himself.*

This would not be the last time Barnabas would advocate for Saul and give him an opportunity to shine. Further, this would not be the only time we see Barnabas boldly believe in and go to bat for others. Later, we will discuss more on the matter of Saul and how the Lord used Barnabas to rescue and redeploy a young man named John Mark. It was Barnabas's continual ministry, gift, and calling to recognize others and set them up for success.

I am eternally grateful to the Barnabas-spirited people who did the same for me in my life. As a young teenager, they encouraged me to be part of mission trips and ministry opportunities in the local church. In fact, our youth minister opened doors for several young people to lead Bible studies among our peers and to teach messages in children's worship.

It was during this season that God began to stir my heart about a lifetime calling to ministry. Church leaders challenged, encouraged, prayed with, and affirmed me at many levels. The fact that others saw ministry potential in me that I could not see in myself was a beautiful example of the powerful Barnabas Spirit that is alive in the Church today!

The Ministry Pipeline Crisis

We are in desperate need of leaders in the Church who, like Barnabas, will recognize the ministry potential in others and advocate for them in the context of the local church. It is a ministry of connecting people who have ministry gifts with ministry opportunities. The current need is massive in most churches both for lay members who will step up and serve and for those specifically called to lead in vocational ministry.

Recent studies sound a warning alarm that a crisis of leadership in the local church is on the horizon. It stems from the ministry pipeline—those responding to the call of God for a life of vocational service in ministry and missions. One study identifies the "aging out" of church leaders as an urgent warning sign. David Kinnamin, president of Barna Research, shares that "there are now more full-time senior pastors over the age of sixty-five than under the age of forty." He concludes, "It is urgent that denominations, networks, and independent churches determine best how to motivate, mobilize, resource, and deploy more younger pastors."[6] The facts are distressing.

Fortunately, several voices are beginning to speak into this great need for calling out leaders to serve in the local church. In their very insightful book, *Calling Out the Called,* authors Scott Pace and Shane Pruitt address the issue at length. They describe these warning signs, writing, "They are blaring alarms of the catastrophic consequences if we fail to address them with anything less than a zealous and concerted effort." Further, they remind church leaders that "we must renew our commitment to 'calling out the called'"![7]

Church leaders can begin to address this great need in their congregations in practical ways. Here are a few ideas to consider:

- Make it a matter of intense personal and corporate prayer.
- Mention the need for laborers to be called into the harvest from the pulpit on a regular basis.
- Create opportunities for students and adults to meet with church leaders and missionaries for fellowship and conversation.
- Discern God-given gifts in young people and adults within the congregation and allow them to teach a class, lead in worship, share a devotional, and experience ministry firsthand.

---

[6] "The Aging of America's Pastors," Barna Group, March 1, 2017, http://barna.com/research/aging-america-pastors.
[7] Scott Pace and Shane Pruitt, *Calling Out the Called,* Scott Pace and Shane Pruitt (B&H Publishing, 2022), 2.

- Develop a residency program or an intern ministry allowing students or young adults an opportunity to serve as part of your church staff for a season to gain personal and practical experience. This can be a volunteer position or funded with a small stipend.

- Include an opportunity to respond to God's call to Christian service as a regular part of the invitation in the message. Encourage the pastor and other ministry leaders to consider making this a priority.

Making a Difference from the Shadows

The kind of ministry that includes going to bat for others and allowing them to experience opportunities for serving the Lord in the local church is truly a behind-the-scenes kind of endeavor. This particular discovery work—indicative of a Barnabas mindset—is what Dr. Jeff Iorg refers to as finding one's "significance in the shadows."[8]

Early in the book, Iorg identifies the term "shadow Christians" as "people who work in dimly lit margins, in the shadows created by the spotlight shining on others. They are believers who serve quietly, often anonymously, doing the work that keeps churches ... functioning." He continues to define these amazing members as making "an impact even when no one knows their name. Their service makes more visible leaders successful."[9]

That is exactly how Barnabas impacted the entire world—he made leaders more visible and useful for ministry! Imagine how this would change the dynamic of your local congregation. It only takes a few godly men and women who begin to practice this kind of impactful ministry to change the spiritual temperature of a church. The ministry of encouragement is not usually listed among the multitude of ministry options on a church's webpage, but it should be prominent in the hearts of the members. It can be cultivated and woven into the fabric of your church.

Perhaps you could begin a Bible study, for example, with a few individuals who exhibit the Barnabas Spirit in your church. This book could serve as a discipleship resource for creating a spirit of encouragement among the members of that small group—or even the congregation at large. Begin today asking the Lord to bring Barnabas-spirited members to your mind and utilize this book if it can be of help in that service.

---

[8] Jeff Iorg, *Shadow Christians*, (B&H Publishing, 2020), 6.
[9] Ibid.

Again, one of the best ways to raise up a Barnabas is to be one. Practice the spirit of Barnabas as an intentional way of modeling the role among your members. Go to bat for others. Give generously with your time, spiritual gifts, and personal resources. God will honor that ministry and multiply it for His glory!

> *One of the best ways to raise up a Barnabas is to be one. Practice the spirit of Barnabas as an intentional way of modeling the role among your members.*

Questions for Discussion

1. How did Barnabas advocate for Saul of Tarsus, and why do you think he did that?

2. In what ways was this a risky move for Barnabas and the Early Church?

3. When and how has anyone ever pushed you into the spotlight of service? How has that positively impacted your ministry in the Church?

4. What concerns related to a crisis of the ministry pipeline are you seeing in the Church? Where are you seeing evidence for concern and how might your church be affected in the future?

5. How can your church begin to address these concerns?

CHAPTER FOUR

Seeing the Grace of God

For the grace of God that brings salvation has appeared to all men . . . (Titus 2:11)

God's grace changes everything. His grace can create masterpieces out of broken pieces. Barnabas knew this truth, and he recognized God's gracious activity when he saw it. In Acts 11, a well-known section of Scripture, we find yet another aspect of Barnabas's character on display. Luke captured it this way: "When he came and had seen the grace of God, he was glad, and encouraged them all that with purpose of heart they should continue with the Lord" (Acts 11:23). Barnabas had the ability and the keen spiritual vision to see God's grace both in individuals and in everyday life situations.

Barnabas, as a result, served as a central figure in one of the most significant movements of God in history. Upon his arrival in Antioch, Barnabas immediately affirmed that God's grace was active and alive among the small band of believers gathered there. The story recorded in Acts 11:19–26 captures a beautiful display of the power of the Gospel and how God used Barnabas to encourage the Church.

The context of the Early Church is stated as being "scattered and persecuted" following the death of Stephen at the hands of the enraged Jewish leaders in Jerusalem (Acts 8:1; Acts 11:19). It was a dangerous season for first-century followers of Jesus, and Antioch was a difficult place. This particular city, known as Antioch of Syria, was the third leading city in the Roman Empire at the time. Perhaps the historian Cicero described Antioch best when he wrote that "Antioch was a place of learned men and luxurious immorality."[10] People were literally running for their lives. Many left their homes and jobs to find safety in faraway places.

Against this backdrop, God was at work. Some of the men who had been persecuted were originally from Cyprus and Cyrene. They landed 300 miles north of Jerusalem in the ancient city of Antioch. As is true most often in God's grace, He takes painful experiences and uses them for His purpose. In this particular situation, God's grace was about to be on full display.

Revival in Unlikely Places

As these persecuted believers arrived in Antioch, they began sharing their story. No doubt, the citizens were interested as these strangers landed ashore and came

---

[10] John MacArthur, *MacArthur New Testament Commentary: Acts 1–12* (Moody Press, 1994), 313.

into the city with very few belongings. So, these new believers shared about Jesus. Initially, they spoke only to the Jewish countrymen, but some eventually began to talk to Gentiles about Christ. They crossed ethnic and cultural boundaries, speaking and preaching about the Lord (Acts 11:20). As they shared the Gospel, they began to chart a new evangelistic and missional course for the Early Church.

They shared their story in the natural flow of conversation, and these unknown and unnamed messengers testified to their hope in Jesus.[11] After all, this was the reason they had fled from Jerusalem in the first place. As new followers of Christ, they were no longer welcome in the Jewish community back home, but they could not keep silent about their Savior!

Residents of Antioch were likely—and apparently—curious about their situation because they listened. Many of these individuals embraced the Lord Jesus themselves. The beautiful words of Acts 11:21 reflect the revival that began in that unlikely place: "And the hand of the Lord was with them, and a great number believed and turned to the Lord."

The evidence of God's grace was obvious even in this unlikely setting. The lyric in an old hymn captures the essence of God's grace in such circumstances: "the vilest offender who truly believes, That moment from Jesus a pardon receives."[12] Ancient Antioch was hardly the kind of place where you would expect to see a great movement of God. Or was it? The Lord has a rich, long, and beautiful history of showing Himself strong in unlikely places and with unworthy people who simply share the Gospel. And then it happened—things began to get out of hand (in the best way), and the number of believers increased rapidly in this unlikely place. God was at work in a difficult setting, during a dangerous season, using an unlikely delivery system!

A Great Place for an Encourager

Largely in part to the efficiency of this young church's "prayer chain"—which is still often a major source of news that travels faster than the speed of light—word about this revival quickly arrived back home in Jerusalem. Something significant was happening in Antioch. People—all kinds of people—were coming to place their trust in Jesus, and in big numbers. In response, the church leaders decided to send big-hearted Barnabas to check things out. Scripture says, "Then news of these things came to the ears of the church in Jerusalem, and they sent out Barnabas to go as far as Antioch" (Acts 11:22).

---

[11] The word translated "spoke" in Greek (and the one used in this context) is a common, conversational verb, not necessarily formal preaching.
[12] Fanny J. Crosby, To God Be the Glory." *The Baptist Hymnal,* (Convention Press, 1956), 41.

They sent Barnabas, the generous guy who always goes to bat for others. And no wonder he was their choice. Luke adds an important bit of commentary on Barnabas's character just a couple verses later: "For he was a good man, full of the Holy Spirit and of faith" (Acts 11:24). That is an epitaph for the ages. Those words are the equivalent of a biblical mic drop in describing this amazing Son of Encouragement.

> *Barnabas's character just a couple verses later: "For he was a good man, full of the Holy Spirit and of faith" (Acts 11:24). That is an epitaph for the ages.*

Upon arriving amid this amazing revival, Barnabas responds in such a beautiful way: "When he came and had seen the grace of God, he was glad, and encouraged them all that with purpose of heart they should continue with the Lord" (Acts 11:23). Barnabas came and he recognized the grace of God. That is such a wonderful, godly characteristic for a church leader to possess.

What this young church in Antioch needed most was to be encouraged and challenged to continue in their ministry. They needed Barnabas to fan the flame of the work of God's grace in their lives. He was exactly the right person at the right time with the right giftings to build up this local body of believers. Barnabas was willing to make the journey and to make a difference with his presence. As a result, the writer Luke adds, "And a great many people were added to the Lord" (Acts 11:24b). Our churches desperately need men and women who will be the Barnabas leaders of this generation to speak life into the body.

Sharing Leadership Roles with Others

Even Barnabas knew when to call for help. As the church in Antioch continued to grow, so did the need for additional leadership. This is one of the key concepts in understanding the power of one person's influence. The simple idea is that no single person can do everything, and we certainly can't do it alone.

One of the significant principles of the Barnabas Spirit is sharing ministry opportunities with others. This may be a "check your ego" moment for some church leaders as they encourage and allow others to serve in their areas of giftedness. It should always be a joyful blessing to see gifted members and leaders thrive as they serve the Lord. It increases the reach of an established leader and expands the ministries of the Church exponentially.

How many churches are limited by the selfish idea that other members are merely spectators and ministry leadership is left to the professionals or to the pastor alone? The bounty of leadership gifts and skillsets often sit untapped in our pews. God's people are woefully underchallenged. Too often churches are lacking volunteers because leaders don't ask or encourage others to get in the game. Members are left on the sidelines when they are so capable of serving in areas of ministry that align with their spiritual gifts. But too many times, ministry leaders fail to recruit others even when the work is overwhelming.

In Acts 11:25–26, the story of Barnabas continues as he enlists the help of Saul of Tarsus. Luke writes, "Then Barnabas departed for Tarsus to seek Saul. And when he had found him, he brought him to Antioch. So it was that for a whole year they assembled with the church and taught a great many people." This was a pivotal moment for the young church at Antioch. They were positioned to do great things for God's Kingdom, but they needed to be discipled. That is the story of every great church.

God's unfolding plan for this ministry opportunity for Saul at Antioch is beautiful to consider, especially since the death of Stephen was directly connected to the persecution that took place. And guess who had been standing right there giving his consent to this horrible moment? Yes, it was none other than this same Saul of Tarsus. Now he was coming to help and not harm. He was brought there to heal and give hope. He was about to be known as Paul the Apostle. But it was because Barnabas saw God's grace and brought him along.

God's grace was extremely evident to those first-century followers of Christ in that unforgettable moment. Barnabas never gave up on Saul. He recognized God's grace, and he understood the power of a changed life. What a lesson for every leader in the Church!

Our church loves to share a story about Ed Newton, who came to us fresh out of college and new to our city to attend seminary in our town. He called the church because he heard we had an opening for a youth ministry intern. We brought Ed onto our staff in a part-time position, but we soon learned that this young man had significant capacity and a unique set of ministry skills.

It wasn't long before Ed became our pastor for young adults and that ministry blossomed. He soon realized a call to serve in full-time evangelism, so he and his wife, Stephanie, took a personal leap of faith and became our staff evangelist—and he served with us for thirteen years. Currently, Dr. Ed Newton serves as the senior pastor of one of the largest churches in America. The most beautiful part of this story is that Ed continues to invest in others and has mentored many young men in ministry. He is always looking for ways to set others up for success!

Here are a few ideas for how this principle can be stirred up and set ablaze in a local church of any size in any context:

- Develop a Barnabas partnership program that encourages every teacher and leader to enlist another person who will serve as their assistant and substitute when they are away. This works well for small group Bible study teachers, children and student ministry workers, building and grounds team members, etc.

- Encourage young people to serve on a special day in worship (Youth Sunday) as they greet, lead prayers, take up the offering, share the music and message, etc. These special services can be planned a few times each year.

  - *Develop partnership*
  - *Encourage young people*
  - *Give opportunity*
  - *Show appreciation*
  - *Share talent/interest*
  - *Encourage church leaders*

- Give new members an opportunity to serve in areas of ministry that need a fresh touch. Enlist, train, and empower others to share in the key areas of leadership.

- Show appreciation for the servant leaders in the congregation who work behind the scenes preparing meals, cleaning the building, and serving the homebound members. Enlist help for these warriors and treat them as heroes of the Church.

- Share a talent/interest survey periodically with the congregation, asking members their top three areas of preference for ministry service in your church. This will at least begin a database for future leaders.

- Encourage church leaders (deacons, elders, teachers, age group workers, etc.) to share their stories on occasion in worship. It can be a simple two-minute video or a platform interview with the pastor. Hearing from others who are on the front lines of ministry often creates a desire in others to also get in the game.

Cultivating Leaders from the Inside

The fact that you are reading this book is evidence that you are hoping to be a Barnabas and likely interested in developing the Barnabas Spirit in your church. I know the joy as a pastor in seeing others thrive in ministry. I've been a part of a church that has chosen to prioritize pouring into young pastors and ministry leaders over the last few decades. We have gladly given away some of our very best for His glory. The Lord has allowed us to see His plan unfold as we simply believed, with God's help, we could reach the whole world with the Gospel!

For me, the Barnabas Spirit is real and personal. I have seen it at work, and I know the value of creating and cultivating this mindset among the members of a church. Don't be discouraged if you currently need additional leaders. Most of our churches can use more workers and servant leaders. Cultivate them from within your congregation. Pray that the Lord of the harvest would send forth laborers (Matthew 9:38 and Luke 10:2)

Questions for Discussion

1. Discuss the negatives, problems, and struggles those believers arriving in Antioch had to deal with. Are there elements of their situation that compare to your church?

2. What impact did the "sharing of their story" have on the citizens of Antioch? How can you encourage your members to begin sharing their Jesus stories?

3. What are the barriers to evangelism and living out our Christian faith that we face as twenty-first century believers, and how can we face those rather than run from them?

4. Who are other unlikely people in history God has used to make a big impact for God's Kingdom?

5. How do you think the Christians at Antioch received Saul of Tarsus and why?

CHAPTER FIVE

Getting in the Game

But he who is greatest among you shall be your servant. And whoever exalts himself will be humbled, and he who humbles himself will be exalted. (Matthew 23:11–12)

Barnabas was a man of humility and faithfulness. He was personally invested and passionately involved in the Lord's work. He served well and sacrificed willingly. Barnabas was not only an encourager, but he was also an example of true servant leadership. He engaged in hands-on work, and he empowered others to get involved. These ancient ideals have never been more needed than now. This Christ-like character quality of Barnabas challenges church leaders in our day to step up to the plate personally for the cause of Christ.

Leading is more than talking about the Christian faith. Authentic leadership is living out the Great Commandments (Matthew 22:36–40) and the Great Commission (Matthew 28:18–20). Barnabas invested his life in the mission enterprise of the Gospel. He not only encouraged others, but he also volunteered and participated in missions personally. We need leaders who get their hands dirty in ministry. We need to get off the sidelines and actually get in the game. This beautiful demonstration by Barnabas is both a practical and profound challenge for the Church in our day.

The Church's First Mission Trip

There came a time when the leaders at Antioch sensed a call to send out missionaries to share the Gospel. Luke shares this beautiful story in Acts 13:2–3: "As they ministered to the Lord and fasted, the Holy Spirit said, 'Now separate to Me Barnabas and Saul for the work to which I have called them.' Then, having fasted and prayed, and laid hands on them, they sent them away." And so began the legend of the first missionary journey of Barnabas and Saul.

Notice that this beautiful moment occurred in the context of worship for this church. The word "ministered" in verse 2 is a worship word. We get our English word "liturgy" from this Greek root. It was also in that moment of worship and in a season of intense, focused prayer that this church became sensitive to the Holy Spirit. They recognized His voice. How many times do we as church leaders fail to hear when the Spirit speaks?

The instructions were simple and clear: Send out or literally "give away" Barnabas and Saul for a particular mission. This church faced a huge opportunity for obedience, but it also involved a great cost. They were being asked to give away their very best leaders. This was no small sacrifice for the young church at Antioch.

Many times, as our church prepared to give away people to help a struggling church or to start a new church, this meant people we loved deeply might leave to follow God's mission for their lives. I was always amazed at the goodness of God in replacing our very best teachers and leaders as we shared with open hands whoever the Lord called away.

On one Sunday morning, I shared a letter from a pastor in a struggling inner-city church in Memphis. He was asking for a few young families to come and attend his church on Sunday mornings. They needed some "ducks on the pond" to help attract and keep young families who might visit their church. I approached the opportunity like a local mission trip for our people and simply asked our members to participate for several months. To my surprise, nearly thirty people responded—including my wife and our three sons. The legend of our generous church family soon became famous on the community grapevine. We became known as "a church that gives people away."

The first time our church launched a new church plant was also a great adventure. We brought a young church planter on to our staff and allowed him to cultivate relationships within the congregation. I remember when the day came for our people to make their commitment to leave and go plant the new church a few miles away in another town. As I stood there that morning to extend the invitation, I was suddenly aware of two fears. The first was, *What if nobody leaves? What if they are too comfortable and aren't willing to go?* My second and greater fear was, *What if everybody leaves?* Of course, those questions are merely humorous, but real feelings surface when a church begins to take such bold steps toward obedience.

That experience of giving away some of our best leaders and most gifted church members allowed our church family to grow in ways we could never have known otherwise. We grew in generosity, sacrifice, and obedience. It was as if the pleasure of God saturated our congregation in such a powerful way. And the Lord began to send more and more people to replace those who left. I will never forget those early days of trusting a great big God to do great big things for His glory!

For the church at Antioch—and for the Church in our day—there is a clear call to obedience. We have similar opportunities to practice the principles of sacrifice and generosity. Just holding the door

> *For the church at Antioch—and for the Church in our day—there is a clear call to obedience.*

for others to walk through is never enough. We must also be ready to invest in the mission through our prayers and our gifts. Each local church, like in Antioch, can be involved by giving financially and providing assistance on many levels. This includes training, providing the supplies, and arranging transportation as needed for the team. The church at Antioch would make provision for these men of God who would literally take the Gospel to the ends of the earth. This first-century church would also be invested in much prayer through this first of its kind mission endeavor.

In Acts 13:1, Luke finally mentions some of the other leaders' names in the church at Antioch. The beautiful mixture of Jewish and Gentile names captures the ethnically diverse nature of this amazing congregation. This church is an example of how the Lord can use anyone in a powerful way who is willing to serve. This small church became a mission outpost of Almighty God with some of the most unlikely people leading the way!

As a pastor, this has been my experience as well. The church I pastored was not the largest or most famous church in town. In fact, there was a long season when we were off the radar completely. Nobody knew about us. But God. And that is always enough. Church leaders should have a measure of confidence that the Lord blesses those who bless Him. But it is not really about our blessing or our boasting. It is very important that we maintain the same spirit of humility that the psalmist proclaimed in Psalm 115:1, "Not unto us, O Lord, not unto us, but to Your name give glory, because of Your mercy, because of Your truth."

Coaching Others

Barnabas was an example of a "player coach" in ministry. He led the church in Antioch from the middle of the pack. He engaged directly in the ministry, and his heart was joyful in sharing leadership roles with others. Barnabas never asked others to do anything that he was not willing to do. His entire life and ministry revolved around personal giving, sharing, going, and serving. But he didn't do it alone. Barnabas enjoyed seeing others become personally involved in the mission.

In his excellent book, *The Coach Model for Christian Leaders*, author Keith Webb addresses this principle. Webb writes, "Those leaders who assign tasks arbitrarily or for their own personal gain 'lord over' their followers. In contrast to this way of leading, Robert Greenleaf coined the term 'servant leadership.'"[13] For Barnabas, this mindset of modeling servant leadership was always on display. He never sought the spotlight personally, but seemed to enjoy seeing others thrive in their areas of ministry calling.

---

[13] Keith E. Webb, *The Coach Model for Christian Leaders* (Morgan James Publishing, 2019), 34.

Webb continues, "Service to others, rather than control, distinguishes servant leaders. Coaching, rather than directing, is an excellent way to serve others. As leaders adopt a coaching approach, they become less autocratic and more empowering, a servant leader."[14] The example of Barnabas is a call to cultivate the spirit of encouragement in the local church. We need leaders who demonstrate sacrifice and service by their personal example. Paul would capture this principle (no doubt learned from Barnabas) when he said, "Imitate me, just as I also imitate Christ" (1 Corinthians 11:1). Imagine the profound impact if every pastor and ministry leader modeled this principle and could say these words with a full measure of conviction!

> *Service to others, rather than control, distinguishes servant leaders. Coaching, rather than directing, is an excellent way to serve others. As leaders adopt a coaching approach, they become less autocratic and more empowering, a servant leader.*

Barnabas mastered this mindset of servant leadership as he encouraged others in the Church. As we have already seen, Barnabas recognized God's grace in others, and he took necessary steps to set them up for success. It might have been easier at times to simply do the work himself, but long-term ministry impact demands sharing leadership roles with others. At the same time, he was never too big or too busy to involve himself personally in the hard work of the ministry. He was always ready to get in the game, and so must we be willing, with God's help.

When Barnabas and Saul were sent out as the first missionaries from the church in Antioch, we see this concept of coaching take shape. The writer Luke introduces the mission team in Acts 13:2 as "Barnabas and Saul." Barnabas was listed first. But that soon changed, and the dynamic duo became known subsequently as "Paul and Barnabas." Paul became the recognized leader. Barnabas had accomplished his coaching mission. And the rest is history.

The Barnabases in My Life

The title of this book, *Everybody Needs a Barnabas,* is the hope in my heart for every believer: to be a Barnabas and to have someone who filled that role in your life. Both are true gifts from God. I've had several role models of the Barnabas Spirit who've impacted my life. These include teachers, coaches, youth ministers, close

---

[14] Ibid.

friends, church leaders, fellow staff members, and pastors. As I share about people in my life who have coached and encouraged me along the way, perhaps the Lord will bring people to mind who have done the same in your life. It is never too late to say "thank you" for these special gifts of God's grace.

Also, think about how you might become more like Barnabas in your ministry setting. Robert Logan reminds us that "being a Barnabas wasn't about Barnabas himself, or what a great difference he could make in the ministry. It was about seeing, affirming, and cooperating with how the Holy Spirit was already at work."[15] He continues with this reminder: "Likewise, if you serve as a Barnabas, it won't be about you. It will be about those you are serving. You're not lording it over others, but coming alongside others, helping them move toward where they sense God leading them."[16] Practicing this principle adds depth and authenticity to our role as leaders in the local church.

> *Being a Barnabas wasn't about Barnabas himself, or what a great difference he could make in the ministry. It was about seeing, affirming, and cooperating with how the Holy Spirit was already at work.*

Early in my Christian faith journey, Nathan and Trish Blackwell came to serve as youth ministry leaders in our church. Nathan was a young seminary student and he, along with his wife, significantly influenced my spiritual growth and maturity during my teen years. Challenging us to memorize Scripture and boldly share our faith, and giving us mission experiences locally and internationally was such a game changer for me and so many of my peers.

It was Nathan who saw potential in my life to become a ministry leader. He coached a group of us to lead in children's worship services and share in youth group meetings. He was instrumental in God's call in my life to ministry as a vocation. Even after I grew up, and they served in another state, we remained in contact—their influence remains powerful to this day. They demonstrated the Barnabas Spirit in our lives.

My first full-time ministry position was in the Orlando area when my wife, Rhonda, and I moved to Trinity Baptist Church in Apopka, Florida. We began a twelve-year season serving as a student pastor and associate pastor alongside Dr. Virgil Lovett and his wife Dianne. Dr. Virg, as I affectionately call him, taught me everything I know about serving as a pastor. He took me with him on hospital and home visits. We talked about preaching and often discussed passages of Scripture and how to

---

[15] Robert E. Logan and Tara Miller, *Becoming Barnabas: A Ministry of Coming Alongside* (Logan Leadership, 2018), 17.
[16] Ibid.

outline them into a sermon. He gave me many opportunities to preach in his pulpit, and he especially trusted me with Sunday nights. He taught me about marriage counseling and funerals and allowed me to share often in those ministries. And now, over forty years later, Dr. Virgil and Ms. Dianne continue to be among our best friends. Their influence in our ministry is immeasurable. They are still Barnabas-like encouragers in our lives, and we will forever be grateful.

As you think about individuals who serve as examples and encouragers in your life, be sure to consider how you can do the same for others. Pour your life into another person by coming alongside them in ministry. Find someone with potential and encourage them to get their hands dirty. Here are a few practical ways to begin coaching and encouraging others:

- Volunteer to lead a local mission project and enlist others to be part of your team.
- Schedule a student-led worship service and select key young people to lead in strategic areas of ministry for the day.
- Begin a Bible reading and Scripture memory club for a few students or young adults.
- Lead your church to read through a chronological Bible and have discussion groups to process the material in a weekly forum.
- Train a small group of younger believers to share their faith and allow them to practice in real life situations.
- Encourage members of all ages to get involved in ministry projects and mission opportunities.

Never Too Late to Get Involved

Sometimes church members get the false notion that they are no longer needed. Perhaps they sense that they have "served their time" and now feel unwanted or otherwise unqualified to serve in some areas of ministry and mission. The church simply doesn't need them anymore, or so it seems. However, nothing could be further from the truth.

Every member is not only needed, but they are also *necessary* for the body to be healthy. Followers of Christ must constantly be encouraged to stay engaged in the ministry and the mission of the Church through every stage of their life. That is one of the primary tasks of the Barnabas ministry in the local church.

It is amazing to see anyone get involved in personal ministry, but it is especially gratifying to see senior adults get in the game and begin to find (or re-find) their mission in life. Many examples of this beautiful awakening occurred in the hearts of our senior saints at the church where I served as pastor for nearly three decades. It was an honor to have a front row seat as the Lord called out people in their later years to significant areas of service.

> *Followers of Christ must constantly be encouraged to stay engaged in the ministry and the mission of the Church through every stage of their life.*

Nina Cole is in heaven now, but what a force for God's Kingdom she became in the last few years of her life! Ms. Nina was a beautiful Southern lady with a distinctive Southern voice to match. On one occasion, she shared her desire to make her life count for the Lord. She told me that she had never led another person to Christ, and she was praying for that to happen. Ms. Nina soon became personally involved in our prison ministry, participated in several mission trips to the Memphis Union Mission, and travelled to Brazil to share the Gospel. She became one of the most effective soul winners in our church. Countless numbers of people trusted Jesus as a result of the faithful obedience of this amazing senior adult lady.

Dr. Teb Bondurant is a retired veterinarian who has a blazing passion for men's ministry in the local church. When Dr. Teb joined our church, it wasn't long before his skillset for this ministry was recognized, and he soon became the men's ministry leader. He brought this ministry to a new level of excellence as our church hosted regional men's conference events and began a weekly gathering on Wednesday evenings called "Man Church." We also continue to host a community men's prayer breakfast every Friday morning at 5:45 a.m. with nearly 100 men attending each week.

Brother James and Mrs. Sandra Williams are another example of a senior couple who found their calling after retiring from successful careers. These dear friends became the mission outpost leaders at the Hope Fellowship ministry that continues to meet inside an apartment complex in the city of Memphis. They provide tutoring for school age children and meet practical needs for families while also leading worship services on Sunday mornings. Their influence for Christ has touched others for more than twenty-five years. They heard about a ministry need and decided to invest their lives in this Kingdom opportunity.

Dr. J.I. Packer discusses the value of senior adults staying engaged in ministry in his excellent book, *Finishing the Course with Joy*. As he refers to the "last lap" for mature believers, he states, "Runners in a distance race, like jockeys in a horse race, always try to keep something in reserve for a final sprint. And my contention is going to be that, so far as our bodily health allows, we should aim to be found running the last lap of the race of our Christian life, as we would say, flat out. The final sprint, so I urge, should be a sprint indeed."[17] Our churches are filled with godly senior adults who need to be challenged to this end!

Questions for Discussion

1. How is role modeling connected to leadership in the Church and why is this important?

2. How is your church capturing the hearts of the next generation's church leaders? What actions are being taken—and how can that be furthered?

3. Who are the Barnabases in your life and how is their influence still making a difference?

4. How is your church celebrating and encouraging senior members who are serving the Lord in missions and ministry?

5. How can a leader who has been on the bench for a while get back in the game in your church?

---

[17] J.I. Packer, *Finishing Our Course with Joy* (Crossway Books, 2014), 21–22.

CHAPTER SIX

When Conflicts Happen

Blessed are the peacemakers, For they shall be called sons of God.
(Matthew 5:9)

Conflicts happen. Good people get twisted with one another. The Church family is no exception to this relational reality—especially in a busy, growing, fast-paced ministry environment. Movement creates friction—and with friction, comes heat.

In Acts 15:36–41, we discover one of the most beautiful moments in the life of Barnabas. It is a reminder that character matters as we share life together in the Lord's work. Ministry is not always smooth, and it is rarely easy. Unfortunate events happen in ministry that can become spiritual wounds, or worse. Conflicts can destroy the unity of a congregation—especially if they are not handled sensitively and in a timely manner.

Luke describes a disagreement between Paul and Barnabas; they ultimately parted ways on two separate missionary teams.

Then after some days Paul said to Barnabas, "Let us now go back and visit our brethren in every city where we have preached the word of the Lord, and see how they are doing." Now Barnabas was determined to take with them John called Mark. But Paul insisted that they should not take with them the one who had departed from them in Pamphylia, and had not gone with them to the work. Then the contention became so sharp that they parted from one another. And so Barnabas took Mark and sailed to Cyprus; but Paul chose Silas and departed, being commended by the brethren to the grace of God. And he went through Syria and Cilicia, strengthening the churches. (Acts 15:36–41)

Disagreements do not have to be disastrous. By God's grace, they can become platforms for planting new Gospel seeds in the fertile soil of new harvest fields. In fact, you may ask the question, "Why do churches and ministries struggle with unity and so often have difficulty getting along?" While sin and selfishness may often be the source of such conflicts, there may also be underlying issues to consider.

> *Why do churches and ministries struggle with unity and so often have difficulty getting along?*

What if our churches become too satisfied with the status quo? Is it possible that some of our churches have grown sinfully comfortable with the way things are?

The Lord is often able to get more accomplished through our failures than we realize. This is true from biblical history. For example, consider Jonah's reluctance to go to Nineveh and how the Lord accomplished His purpose despite Jonah's initial disobedience. Or what about Joseph and the sibling rivalry that resulted in God's deliverance of Israel? How many lessons can we learn from David's failures and God's faithfulness in his life?

Never Give Up on People

The church at Antioch commended Paul and Silas, but the Lord also used Barnabas and John Mark in a profound way. In this moment, the Apostle Paul seemed to be giving up on a young man for his temporary failure. John Mark had been sent home early on the first missionary journey. Details are limited (Acts 13:13), but scholars have suggested some things about the young man's departure in Pamphylia. Perhaps John Mark became ill and needed medical attention. Or maybe he simply became homesick and needed to head back to his family in Jerusalem.

Either way (or for a number of other reasons), Paul dismissed the young missionary as someone who could not be trusted or was not useful for this journey. History would prove that Paul was wrong. He would later admit his misjudgment in a very heart-stirring way. Later in his life, Paul would invite Mark to come visit him in prison. That bit of Scripture is very telling as Paul writes, "Only Luke is with me. Get Mark and bring him with you, for he is useful to me for ministry" (2 Timothy 4:11). Time often provides great wisdom and perspective to relationships in life.

In a beautiful turn of events, God used the shortcomings of young John Mark to produce blessings for the Church that remain to this day. Barnabas believed in John Mark. He was able to see with spiritual eyes and discernment that God had a plan for the young man. Most scholars agree that it was this same John Mark who would later write the Gospel of Mark.

Think for a moment about your own failures in the ministry. Has there ever been a time when you felt like quitting or at least considered getting out for a season? Are there people who dismissed you for your lack of experience or for some failure to meet expectations? If so, please take heart and be encouraged by this Barnabas principle. God never gives up on His people. Certainly, there are seasons of suffering and consequences for sin, but the Lord is faithful to bring to completion the good work that He has begun in your life (Philippians 1:6).

One of the powerful lessons learned from Barnabas is to never give up on people. I'm so thankful that I had men in my life who saw my potential and recognized that spiritual growth and maturity were possible. God placed several men in my path who never gave up on me. Let us do the same for others. Let us be reminded not to give up on others too quickly. We all need a measure of grace along the way. There are likely members in our churches who have given up on themselves. They need a Barnabas to come along and recognize their potential to serve the Lord!

The Faith Baptist Church Story

I had the privilege of serving as the first full-time pastor for Faith Baptist Church in Bartlett, Tennessee. I served in that role for more than twenty-seven years. In fact, it is the only church where I ever served as senior pastor. Most of my adult life, I had the honor of loving, leading, and shepherding this amazing congregation. Faith Baptist Church grew into one of the most Kingdom-focused and mission-driven churches in our state. The church still has a heart for helping struggling churches, starting new churches and ministries, and sending laborers in the harvest. But it didn't begin that way.

Faith Baptist was born from a wound. More than three decades ago, another church in our town went through a leadership conflict. Good people, many who were lifetime and long-term members, were deeply hurt. Friendships became stressed and families were fractured. As a result, hundreds of members walked away. They dispersed and became members of several other churches in the area.

On an occasion, one of the former Sunday school classes planned a fellowship in a local community center to reconnect with old friendships. Someone noted at that meeting that this group was large enough to start a new church. And the idea was born that eventually became a new church plant from previous pain. Interestingly, the church that had split had never planted a new church in its more than 150-year-old history. The analogy I've often used is that of a church being pregnant with an unwanted child. But God had another plan.

The idea of serving as pastor of a church split was the furthest thing from my ministry goals. In fact, I've often said about the early beginnings of Faith that I was "minding my own business in sunny Central Florida and I had nothing to do with this conflict." I can tell you that it is not easy serving a wounded congregation. I found out quickly that leadership trust for the pastor has to be earned—it cannot merely be assumed. Wounded people are wary of strong leaders and need to be carefully and gently led along.

By the grace of God, Faith became a healthy church family despite the difficult beginning and the pain that was etched into its history. The church recognized that we had been given a great responsibility to see the community healed and to become a church that advanced God's Kingdom on purpose. Our church family still has a strong desire to make much of Jesus and to live out God's mission as a healthy, reproducing congregation.

When a new pastor came to serve the other congregation in town, we were able to leverage our friendship to begin the healing process. We shared in a community Thanksgiving service bringing our congregations back together for fellowship and healing. It was the beginning of a process that has helped our churches partner together and protect the good name of Jesus in our community. A wound became a blessing. As a result, many new churches have been planted and others strengthened along the way.

Following the Biblical Pattern

The word *reconciliation* is a significant concept in Scripture. For example, in 2 Corinthians, Paul refers to the fact that "God was in Christ reconciling the world to Himself, not imputing their trespasses to them, and has committed to us the word of reconciliation" (2 Corinthians 5:19). To *reconcile* means to bring things back in balance or to reconnect things that were once broken. That is exactly what the Barnabas Spirit can do in the local church. Just as John Mark was eventually brought back into ministry and his relationship with Paul was reconnected, so God has called each of us to the task of reconciliation.

In the context of the local church, there are doubtless many relationships that have become disconnected or otherwise wounded. Who can address these things, if not for a Barnabas brother or sister within the church family? It is such a beautiful moment when God's people follow the biblical pattern for coming back together in love and forgiveness.

Apparently, this is a lesson Paul learned from Barnabas that he never forgot. On several occasions, Paul refers to this idea of healing and reconciliation in the Church. For instance, in Ephesians he writes, "Let all bitterness, wrath, anger, clamor, and evil speaking be put away from you, with all malice. And be kind to one another, tenderhearted, forgiving one another, even as God in Christ forgave you" (Ephesians 4:31–32). I love the humility and deference in these words that reflect the Barnabas Spirit in such a powerful and practical way.

Likewise, in Colossians, Paul writes a similar admonition to the church. He says, "Therefore, as the elect of God, holy and beloved, put on tender mercies, kindness, humility, meekness, longsuffering; bearing with one another, and forgiving one another, if anyone has a complaint against another; even as Christ forgave you, so you also must do" (Colossians 3:12–13). Perhaps even at this moment while you are reading these words, the Lord is bringing to mind a friendship or relationship that needs healing.

Here are a few steps to consider when addressing wounded relationships in the Church:

- Saturate the situation with prayer.
- Keep in mind that not everyone wants to participate in the hard work of healing. In such cases, cover the process with prayer. Be patient and find ways to open communication without causing further conflict.

- Early on, it may be easier to begin the process of healing by writing a personal letter and waiting for a response.
- Be sure you have the mindset and spirit of humility as you approach another person in this process.
- Remember that every person has their own pace and frame of reference for healing.
- Be patient and trust the Lord to touch the other person's heart.
- Accept your role in the disagreement or misunderstanding openly and honestly.
- Confess with a broken heart your sorrow and ask forgiveness as the situation determines.
- Keep on praying and pursuing reconciliation—it is worth it!

Reconciliation is Worth it

When God's people begin to practice this Barnabas principle, the Church will become healthier and more spiritually vibrant. There is humility and spiritual depth that accompanies such healing within a congregation. It sends a powerful message to the watching world when the Church engages in reconciliation. Partnership and fellowship can be restored between individuals and churches. Let us give our lives to this great challenge. Life is too short, and God is too good, for us to remain at odds with our brothers and sisters in Christ. Jesus can help us if we trust Him.

Questions for Discussion

1. In modern times, how is Paul and John Mark's conflict duplicated? Why do you think it happens so often?

2. Discuss the scenario and possible outcomes if Barnabas had not believed in John Mark—and think about the consequences for the Church.

3. Write down the people who believed in you along the way in your Christian journey. How does their Barnabas Spirit impact the way you treat others?

4. Discuss real-life situations where churches or church members have become wounded in their relationships. Use your imagination and share scenarios that could result in such conflicts or wounds in a church.

5. Share practical ways believers can practice reconciliation. Read Matthew 18:15–17 and discuss the biblical steps mentioned in this process for healing.

38

CHAPTER SEVEN

Jesus, Our Ultimate Encourager

For even the Son of Man did not come to be served, but to serve, and to give His life a ransom for many. (Mark 10:45)

Jesus is the ultimate encourager. His entire life exemplified sacrifice and service to others. That's why Paul could say, "Let this mind be in you which was also in Christ Jesus" (Philippians 2:5). Jesus is the perfect model to emulate for humility, generosity, and caring for others. When Jesus described Himself in Scripture, He did so with this beautiful invitation: "Come to Me, all you who labor and are heavy laden, and I will give you rest. Take My yoke upon you and learn from Me, for I am gentle and lowly in heart, and you will find rest for your souls. For My yoke is easy and My burden is light" (Matthew 11:28–30).

These words have served to encourage believers and lift their burdens for generations. Jesus understands the weight and the burdens humans carry. He invites us into "rest" that is more than temporary ease—it also includes lasting comfort in body, soul, and spirit. Jesus offers the ultimate peace, one that truly surpasses all human understanding. He promised that we could "be of good cheer" in the midst of life's storms because He has "overcome the world" (John 16:33).

Barnabas learned to follow His example, and he demonstrated the character of Christ beautifully throughout his life. It was a process over time, but he was truly a Christ follower. Every principle we have discussed in this small book has the life of Jesus as its foundation. By studying the life of Barnabas, it has been my goal to connect all his character qualities and attributes directly to the Lord Jesus—our ultimate encourager.

Jesus is God in human flesh who dwelt among us. He is the *Logos* who entered our human experience. Jesus touched the putrid flesh of lepers, and He spoke kindly to guilty sinners. His life of generosity, sacrifice, patience, and seeing the best in others is beyond legendary. Without a strong connection to Jesus, no person or church can survive in this discouraging world. With a clear focus and commitment to Jesus, however, believers and their churches can thrive as they seek to demonstrate and communicate these life-giving principles to others.

Jesus saw potential in a band of fishermen (Matthew 4:18–22), tax collectors (Matthew 9:9), and zealots (Luke 6:15). He never gave up on Peter, and He hasn't given up on you. Jesus will never give up on His Church as He continues to build her strong and beautiful in every generation. It is my hope and prayer that the life of Barnabas, as he modeled Jesus, will serve to stir a fresh ministry focus in your heart and ignite spiritual fire in the life of your congregation. It is my prayer that the principles in this book will help to cultivate a spirit of encouragement in your congregation that will last for generations.

In most of my sermons, I usually quote a line or two from an old hymn. They encourage my soul and often shine light on a particular point or principle I'm trying to make. One of those old hymns came to mind as I was writing this final chapter on Jesus—our ultimate encourager. I hope these words will bless you as they have blessed me as I visited them anew. The hymn is "What a Friend We Have in Jesus." The author, Joseph Scriven, gave us this beautiful reminder of the encouraging nature of our Savior:

What a friend we have in Jesus, All our sins and griefs to bear!

What a privilege to carry Ev'rything to God in prayer!

Oh, what peace we often forfeit, Oh, what needless pain we bear,

All because we do not carry Ev'rything to God in prayer!

Have we trials and temptations? Is there trouble anywhere?

We should never be discouraged, Take it to the Lord in prayer:

Can we find a friend so faithful Who will all our sorrows share?

Jesus knows our ev'ry weakness, Take it to the Lord in prayer.[18]

A Name Like No Other

Jesus is the most beautiful name in the Bible. It is the name that brings salvation. Peter and John proclaim that "there is no other name under heaven given among men by which we must be saved" (Acts 4:12). Jesus is also the name that is above all others. Paul affirms that God has "given Him the name which is above every name, that at the name of Jesus every knee should bow, of those in heaven and those on earth, and of those under the earth, and that every tongue should confess that Jesus Chris is Lord, to the glory of God the Father" (Philippians 2:9–11).

Barnabas was commonly known by his nickname as the "Son of Encouragement." Even though Jesus has been known by many lovely titles and names, the name He most often refers to Himself in the Gospels is "the Son of Man." This particular title is rooted in Old Testament prophecy. It foretold the humble nature of the promised

---

[18] Joseph Scriven, "What a Friend We Have in Jesus." *The Baptist Hymnal*, (Convention Press, 1956), 328.

Messiah who would come as a suffering servant. Charles Spurgeon eloquently explains how we are to learn humility from Jesus. He writes:

Let us learn a lesson of humility from our Saviour; let us never court great titles or proud degrees. If Jesus called himself the Son of Man, when he had far greater names, let us learn to humble ourselves unto men of low estate, knowing that he that humbleth himself shall in due time be exalted. Jesus Christ called himself the Son of Man, because he loved to be a man. It was a great stoop for him to come from heaven and to be incarnate. But condescension though it was, he loved it.[19]

> Let us learn a lesson of humility from our Saviour; let us never court great titles or proud degrees.

Grace So Amazing

God's grace in the sacrifice of Jesus is the ultimate act of generosity. There has never been a more costly gift or a more unworthy recipient than sinful humanity. The perfect, sinless Son of God suffered and bled and died for our sins. No wonder John the Baptist would declare this legendary introduction of Jesus, "Behold! The Lamb of God who takes away the sin of the world" (John 1:29). In that concise sentence, John captured the entire essence of the Gospel.

When he referred to Jesus as the Lamb of God, every Jewish person in earshot knew exactly the connection he was making. Reaching all the way back to the Garden of Eden when God made coats of skin for Adam and Eve, this language was clear (Genesis 3:21). It echoes through the story of Abraham offering his son Isaac and that God would "provide for Himself the lamb" (Genesis 22:8). The illustration of the lamb permeates the Jewish sacrificial system. Jesus is the ultimate sacrifice for our sins: the Lamb of God. The writer of Hebrews would remind us of this truth: "But Christ came as High Priest of the good things to come, with the greater and more perfect tabernacle not made with hands, that is, not of this creation. Not with the blood of goats and calves, but with His own blood He entered the Most Holy Place once for all, having obtained the eternal redemption" (Hebrews 9:11–12).

Ultimately, John would capture the culmination of this grace in the well-known verse which eloquently states, "For God so loved the world that He gave His only begotten Son, that whoever believes in Him should not perish, but have everlasting life" (John 3:16). John's declaration is a beautiful reminder that anyone who places their faith in Jesus can be saved. God's grace is sufficient. This is God's extravagant gift to broken mankind. Jesus is the only way. He would make this very clear when He said, "I am the way, the truth, and the life. No one comes to the Father except through me" (John 14:6).

---

[19] Charles Haddon Spurgeon, *Spurgeon's Sermons*, vol. 6, (Baker Book House, 1985), 92–93.

The Apostle Paul never got over his encounter with God's amazing grace. In several accounts of Scripture, he shared his testimony of being a fiery religious zealot who was hostile toward followers of Jesus until that day on the road to Damascus when everything changed. In that moment of coming face to face with the resurrected Lord Jesus, Paul surrendered everything to Christ. He no longer counted his pedigree or prideful accomplishments as anything but trash. His one flaming desire and passion was to follow Jesus and proclaim the Gospel. It was God's grace that created this legendary change in Paul's life. Here is the declaration in Paul's own words:

But what things were gain to me, these I have counted loss for Christ. Yet indeed I also count all things loss for the excellence of the knowledge of Christ Jesus my Lord, for whom I have suffered the loss of all things, and count them as rubbish, that I may gain Christ and be found in Him, not having my own righteousness, which if from the law, but that which is through faith in Christ, the righteousness which is from God by faith; that I may know Him and the power of His resurrection, and the fellowship of His sufferings, being conformed to His death, if, by any means, I may attain to the resurrection from the dead. (Philippians 3:7–11)

Jesus Humbled Himself Like No Other

One of the accusations levied against Jesus by the religious elite of His day was that he was a friend of sinners. (Luke 15:2). We can all be grateful that He still is. His whole life was marked by this reality as He journeyed toward the cross. He spoke to the speechless, gave sight to the blind, set the guilty free from their bondage, and gave hope to the hopeless. He still does—and He invites us into this "get your hands dirty" kind of ministry.

The Christian faith was never intended to be all talk and no action. It is not about ivory tower religious expressions that fit nicely on our coffee cups. Jesus has invited His people to touch the untouchable, go to dangerous places, and love the unlovely. His life serves as a prime example of this kind of ministry. It was His mission, and it must become ours if we are ever going to impact the lostness in our generation.

> *Jesus has invited His people to touch the untouchable, go to dangerous places, and love the unlovely. His life serves as a prime example of this kind of ministry.*

As I have been invited to preach in various churches in recent years, I have noticed that some of our congregations grasp this truth more than others. In some places, there are scuffs on the wall and stains on the carpet from active ministries to children and young people. Other churches have no noise from the nursery and immaculate buildings with no stains. For me, I prefer the scuffs of ministry in churches that get their hands dirty and do whatever it takes to reach people young and old. We are called to make disciples of all people, and there is a cost associated with such commitment. Sometimes this kind of ministry gets messy!

The Barnabas Spirit is all about following the example of Jesus. Just as Jesus found it necessary to go through Samaria and to encounter the woman at the well (John 4), so must we be willing to cross barriers that distract and divide us. We must always show compassion and grace to people who are in need. Jesus loves all people. So must we.

Questions for Discussion

1. How was the life of Barnabas impacted by Jesus's example of giving and generosity?

2. What similarities can you see between the character qualities in Barnabas as compared to Jesus?

3. Write down other examples of Jesus showing love and respect for hurting and wounded people in the stories from the Gospels.

4. In what ways does your church engage in the messy things of ministry in your community?

5. How can you encourage your church leaders and members to become more personally involved in reaching the lost?

Epilogue

The story of Barnabas is still being written. His influence continues through the lives of ordinary believers who love to encourage others. Chances are, you are one of those unique individuals who possesses the Barnabas Spirit. This is often a behind the scenes ministry that is rarely noticed or acknowledged publicly. But the Lord knows—and He is honored by your willingness to push others into the spotlight of missions and ministry. On behalf of generations who have been influenced by a Barnabas, I say, "Thank you!"

There are countless others sitting in our churches who need to be encouraged. We will always have plenty of opportunities to speak words of life into people. May the Lord continue to use leaders like Barnabas to see the grace of God, go to bat for others, and invest their lives in His eternal Kingdom. Who knows—there may be a few more Saul of Tarsus and John Mark leaders waiting to be encouraged!

One of the hopes in my heart as I wrote this book was for it to serve as a reminder of the power of Chrisitan encouragement in the local church. If this power could be harnessed and unleashed among God's people, imagine how healthy our churches would become. There may never be an award for encouraging others in our trophy case here on earth, but heaven will have some MVP awards waiting for believers who practice the Barnabas Spirit in everyday life.

Please know that your life matters and your godly influence as an encourager is greatly valued in the grand story of God's work in the world. May the words of Fanny J. Crosby encourage you along the way: "Great things he hath taught us, great things he hath done, And great our rejoicing thro' Jesus the Son; But purer, and higher, and greater will be Our wonder, our vict'ry, when Jesus we see!"[20]

---

[20] Fanny J. Crosby, "To God Be the Glory." *The Baptist Hymnal,* (Convention Press, 1956), 41.

Acknowledgments

To my best friend and Barnabas for life—my wife, Rhonda. Thank you for your constant encouragement in our journey of ministry and sharing life together!

To my friend and encourager, Tom Day—thank you for reading the unedited version of these pages and offering your valuable ideas and insights!

To our amazing media and communications team at the Tennessee Baptist Mission Board— thank you for making this project happen!

To a lifetime of godly men and women in churches where I attended and served— the Lord knows the value of your influence in my life!

To my pastor brothers who serve on the frontlines every single day—your faithfulness and godly shepherding of the Bride encourages me beyond words!

To all the wonderful staff and colleagues that I have the privilege of calling friends in the ministry—my life is better because of your encouragement along the way!

To my three amazing sons and our seven beautiful grandchildren—I love being your Dad and Papa the most!

Made in the USA
Coppell, TX
29 December 2025

67827777R00036